Conversation Starters
for

Fredrik Backman's

And Every Morning the Way Home Gets Longer and Longer

By dailyBooks

  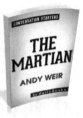

Tips for Using dailyBooks Conversation Starters:

EVERY GOOD BOOK CONTAINS A WORLD FAR DEEPER THAN the surface of its pages. The characters and their world come alive through the words on the pages, yet the characters and its world still live on. Questions herein are designed to bring us beneath the surface of the page and invite us into the world that lives on. These questions can be used to:

- Foster a deeper understanding of the book
- Promote an atmosphere of discussion for groups
- Assist in the study of the book, either individually or corporately
- Explore unseen realms of the book as never seen before

About Us:

THROUGH YEARS OF EXPERIENCE AND FIELD EXPERTISE, from newspaper featured book clubs to local library chapters, *dailyBooks* can bring your book discussion to life. Host your book party as we discuss some of today's most widely read books.

Table of Contents

Introducing *And Every Morning the Way Home Gets Longer and Longer*

IN *AND EVERY MORNING THE WAY HOME GETS LONGER AND Longer,* a young boy named Noah interacts with his grandfather whose memory is failing. The novel begins with Grandpa and Noah sitting next to one another. Grandpa expresses that he does not want to forget. Noah tells him not to be afraid and tries to be brave himself. Noah and Grandpa recite the numbers of pi together in an attempt to help them both find courage. Grandpa explains to Noah that his memory is failing by telling him the square in his brain is getting smaller.

After the interaction with Noah, the scene flashes back to an earlier time in Grandpa's memory. This time he is with his son, Ted. Ted excels in reading and language, but he struggles in mathematics. Ted refuses to recite the numbers of pi with Grandpa. Grandpa is confused by this which causes him to become angry with Ted. Suddenly, Ted tells Grandpa that he is bleeding. The scene returns again to the present time. Ted is there telling Grandpa that he is bleeding and should sit down.

Later in the story, Grandpa is bleeding again. This time Noah is there and informs him of his condition. Noah asks if it is time for them to learn to tell each other goodbye. Grandpa tells him that as much as he doesn't want it to be true, it is time. Noah reflects on their goodbyes in the past. Noah recalls that his grandfather would not let him say goodbye when they would visit in the past. Noah tells Grandpa that saying goodbye is hard for him. Grandpa takes his hands and reassures him that there will be many times they can practice saying goodbye now. Noah notices that Grandpa is gripping his hand tightly and asks him why. Grandpa tells him that it feels as though everything is rapidly disappearing from his world, and he wants Noah to be the person he holds on to the longest. Grandpa's memory flashes back to a time when he was a teenager. He is with Grandma again.

Toward the end of the story, Grandpa tells Noah that after he is able to say the perfect goodbye, he must say it and never turn back. He makes Noah promise he won't look back and move forward to live his life. Noah tells Grandpa that if he ever forgets him, he will have the chance to get to know him all over again.

Introducing the Author

IN JUNE OF 1981, FREDRIK BACKMAN WAS BORN IN Sweden. As a young child, he spent much of his time near the city of Helsinki, Sweden. Prior to his career as a novelist, he drove a forklift in a factory that produced fruits and vegetables. One day, while at work, he was struck with the idea that he could write stories and receive payment for them. At this point, he decided he would take writing more seriously. Before turning writing into a career, Backman wrote for publications and did not receive payment for them. After writing for free for several months, Backman was offered a job writing for two magazines – *Moore Magazine* and *Helginsborg Dagblad*.

To support himself financially while writing his first novel, Backman had to work for fourteen hours a day over the weekend. During the week, Backman would work on writing his novel. This was his routine for one year. In 2012, his first novel, *A Man Called Ove*, was published. After its publication in Sweden, *A Man Called Ove* was published in over thirty more countries. Backman's breakthrough with his first novel allowed him to work full time as a writer. When Backman published *A Man Called Ove*, he also received an advance payment for a second novel from his publisher.

Backman's second novel is titled *Saker min son behöver veta om världen*. It was released in 2012, as well, and it was never translated to English. His third novel is titled *My Grandmother Asked Me to Tell You She's Sorry*, and it was published in 2013. In 2014, Backman's fourth novel, *Britt-Marie was here* was released. In 2016, Backman published the novella *And Every Morning the Way Home Gets Longer and Longer*. Backman admits he never intended for his novel to be read by the public. However, he decided to publish the story anyway. His latest novel, *Beartown*, is set to be published in 2017.

Discussion Questions

. . . .

question 1

Grandpa is a elderly man who is losing his memory. Compare Grandpa at the
beginning of the story and at the end of the story. How did he change
throughout the story?

. . . .

● GPA CAN RECITE PI

     ↳

● HAS CONDITION HE FORGOT
ABOUT → BLEEDING ?

question 2

Fredrick Backman's novel *And Every Morning the Way Home Gets Longer and Longer,* centers around the topic of Alzheimer's, Dementia, and aging. What do you think Backman's purpose was in writing about this topic?

question 3

It seems as though Grandpa and Ted had a rocky relationship at first because they had different interests. Compare the relationship between Grandpa and Ted when Ted was a young boy to their relationship when Ted was an adult. How has their relationship evolved?

question 4

And Every Morning the Way Home Gets Longer and Longer often switches between Grandpa's life in the present day and his life in the past. Why do you think the author chose to write this story with changing time periods?

. . . .

question 5

Aging parents and grandparents and memory loss are often difficult for
families to deal with. Do you think the author was trying to send any message
to the reader by writing this story?

. . . .

· ·

question 6

Grandpa is losing his memory quickly. Despite this, his family stays by his side and continues to visit him. Why do you think they made the choice to continue to visit him?

· ·

. . . .

question 7

Grandpa makes Noah promise that once he has perfected his goodbye that he will never look back and move forward with his life. Why do you think Grandpa has Noah make this promise?

. . . .

. . . .

question 8

Noah's grandfather makes him promise that he will move forward and not look back after he has learned to say the perfect goodbye. Do you think it is possible for Noah to learn to say the perfect goodbye? If he could, do you think it is possible for him to never look back?

. . . .

. . . .

question 9

Mathematics is a common theme in this story. What role does Mathematics play in this story?

. . . .

question 10

One of this author's novels has been adapted to film. If *And Every Morning the Way Home Gets Longer and Longer* were adapted to film, as well, how do you think the novel would translate as a film?

. . . .

question 11

Compare the relationship between Noah and Grandpa at the beginning of the novel to the end of the novel. How does their relationship grow or change as the novel progresses?

. . . .

. . . .

question 12

And Every Morning the Way Home Gets Longer and Longer follows a family who is watching the patriarch's memory fade away. Is this story driven more by the plot or the characters in the story?

. . . .

question 13

Consider the character of Noah. How does he evolve throughout the course of the novel?

question 14

Many of Grandpa's memories involve his wife and the times they shared together. The only information the reader has of Grandma is through the perspective of Grandpa's memories. Why do you think the author chose to include the character of Grandma in this why? Why do you think Grandma shows up in so many of Grandpa's memories?

. . . .

question 15

What were your thoughts on how this story ended? Were you expecting the story to end in the way it did, or were you surprised?

. . . .

. . . .

question 16

Readers of *And Every Morning the Way Home Gets Longer and Longer* have stated that the novel made them cry. What was your reading experience?

. . . .

. . . .

question 17

Fredrik Backman's portrayal of elderly people in his novels is superb in the opinion of one reader. How did you find Backman's portrayal of an aging person in this novel?

. . . .

. . . .

question 18

Many readers commented on Fredrik Backman's ability to tell a moving story in less than one hundred pages. What were your thoughts on the length of this novel?

. . . .

. . . .

question 19

Alzheimer's, Dementia, and aging parents or grandparents are subject that are
familiar to many readers of this novel. What is your experience with these
topics? How true-to-life was Backman with these topics?

. . . .

question 20

According to readers of *And Every Morning the Way Home Gets Longer and Longer*, Fredrik Backman has created a unique story. What sets this story apart from others you have read?

FREE Download: Bonus Books Included
*Claim Yours with **Any Purchase** of* Conversation Starters!

  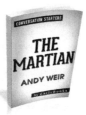

How to claim your free download:

4. <u>**LEAVE MY AMAZON REVIEW.**</u>
You Can Also Use "Write a Customer Review" Button

5. <u>**ENTER YOUR BEST EMAIL HERE.**</u>
NO SPAM. Your Email is Never Shared and is Protected

Or Scan Above

6. **RECEIVE YOUR FREE DOWNLOAD.**
Download is Instantly Delivered to Inbox

question 21

In the opinion of one reader, Fredrik Backman is able to tell a story that makes the reader feel as though they know the characters personally. What was your opinion of the characters in this novel?

. . . .

question 22

One reader found *And Every Morning the Way Home Gets Longer and Longer* to be confusing and hard to follow. What were your thoughts on the changing time periods throughout the novel?

. . . .

. . . .

question 23

Readers have compared *And Every Morning the Way Home Gets Longer and Longer* to authors such as Mitch Albom and Emma Healey. Which stories or authors, if any, does this novel remind you of?

. . . .

. . . .

question 24

And Every Morning the Way Home Gets Longer and Longer has an average rating of 4.5 out of 5 stars on Goodreads, Amazon, and Barnes & Noble. What rating would you give this novel?

. . . .

. . . .

question 25

Heartbreaking, heartwarming, beautiful, winsome, and wise were all words used to describe *And Every Morning the Way Home Gets Longer and Longer*. What words would you use to describe this novel?

. . . .

. . . .

question 26

Fredrik Backman has made it known that he never wanted the public to read *And Every Morning the Way Home Gets Longer and Longer.* Why do you think he published this title anyway?

. . . .

. . . .

question 27

There is one novel by Backman that was never translated into English. Why
do you think this novel was not translated?

. . . .

. . . .

question 28

Fredrik Backman had a steady job and income as a forklift driver. Why do you think he chose to take the risk and become a full-time novelist?

. . . .

question 29

As he was writing his first novel, Fredrik Backman worked fourteen hour days every weekend. He worked on his novel during the week. What are your thoughts on Backman's routine during this time?

. . . .

question 30

If you were able to sit down with Fredrik Backman and interview him, what questions would you ask him?

. . . .

. . . .

question 31

Even though Grandpa is losing his memory, his family stays by his side and continues to visit him. How might the story be different if they had chosen not to visit Grandpa as his memory declined?

. . . .

. . . .

question 32

If you had the chance to sit down and talk with any character in the novel,
who would you choose? What questions would you ask them?

. . . .

question 33

Imagine that you were in Noah's position. How would you handle your grandparent's failing memory?

. . . .

question 34

If you had the ability to change any one part of this story, which part would
you choose to change? Why would you change that part of the story?

. . . .

. . . .

question 35

And Every Morning the Way Home Gets Longer and Longer is told from a
third-person perspective. How might the story change if it were told from a
first-person point of view?

. . . .

question 36

This story follows a family who must learn to let go of their ailing father and grandfather. How might the story be different if Noah or Ted were the characters whose heath was failing instead of Grandpa?

. . . .

question 37

Grandpa seems to have difficulty explaining to Noah and allowing Noah to let him go. If you were in Grandpa's place, what would you say to Noah to comfort him through this difficult time?

. . . .

. . . .

question 38

Noah tries to help Grandpa remember as much as he can. However, every day Grandpa loses more of his memories. If you were Noah, what would you do or say to help Grandpa as his memory continues to fail?

. . . .

Quiz Questions

. . . .

question 39

In *And Every Morning the Way Home Gets Longer and Longer*,
_____ is losing his memory.

. . . .

question 40

_____ and Grandpa share a love of Mathematics. They often sit together and discuss the topic.

question 41

Grandpa and _____ have always had different interests. Grandpa, who loved Mathematics, found it hard to bond with him because he was interested in words and music.

question 42

Grandpa tells Noah that as soon as he learns to say the perfect
_____, he must move forward and never look back.

. . . .

question 43

True or False: The square is a symbol of Grandpa's memory. Every day, the square gets smaller as Grandpa's memory gets smaller.

. . . .

question 44

True or False: Grandpa tells Noah that he is holding onto his hand tightly because he wants to hold on to Noah the longest.

question 45

True or False: Noah knows it will be easy for him to say goodbye to Grandpa. He is sure that he will see Grandpa again in Heaven.

. . . .

question 46

The author of *And Every Morning the Way Home Gets Longer and Longer* is named Fredrik _____.

. . . .

question 47

The author was born in _____ and spent much of his
childhood in the city of Helsinki.

. . . .

question 48

True or False: Before becoming a novelist, the author drove a forklift in a fruit and vegetable factory.

. . . .

question 49

True or False: The author's first novel was released in 2014 and titled *Britt-Marie Was Here.*

. . . .

question 50

True or False: The author was excited for the public to read *And Every Morning the Way Home Gets Longer and Longer* as soon as he started writing the story.

. . . .

Quiz Answers

1. Grandpa
2. Noah
3. Ted
4. Goodbye
5. True
6. True
7. False, Noah struggles with saying goodbye to Grandpa.
8. Backman
9. Sweden
10. True
11. False, his first novel was *A Man Called Ove,* which was released in 2012.
12. False, he never intended for the story to be read by the public.

THE END

Want to promote your book group?
Register here.

PLEASE LEAVE US A FEEDBACK.

THANK YOU!

FREE Download: Bonus Books Included
*Claim Yours with **Any Purchase** of* Conversation Starters!

  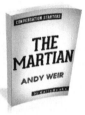

How to claim your free download:

7. <u>**LEAVE MY AMAZON REVIEW.**</u>
You Can Also Use "Write a Customer Review" Button

8. <u>**ENTER YOUR BEST EMAIL HERE.**</u>
NO SPAM. Your Email is Never Shared and is Protected

Or Scan Above

9. **RECEIVE YOUR FREE DOWNLOAD.**
Download is Instantly Delivered to Inbox

Made in the USA
Middletown, DE
27 May 2022